CW00820415

THE GYPSY,
THE TINKER AND THE
TRAVELLING MAN

Compiled by John McKale

Published by John McKale

Copyright © John McKale 2015

First published 2015

By the same publisher

The Tilly Wood Story, extracts from the life of a Romany Gypsy, 2009
The Gypsies Then and Now, Life Among Gypsies and Travellers, 2009
Gypsy Life in Britain, Past and Present, 2010
A Century of British Gypsies, 2012
Gypsy Wagon Painters, 2013

Edited by Rob Bulmer

No part of this book may be reproduced, stored in a retrieval system or transmitted in any
form, or by any means electronic, mechanical, photocopying, recording or otherwise
without the prior permission of the Publisher and the copyright holders.

For further information contact John McKale
07769660194 / 0191 2673152
email: mckale@blueyonder.co.uk

Printed by

ISBN 978-0-9562266-5-5

Dedicated to my dear wife Veronica and
family

Also to the memory of
Clara (Mudsey) Barras
and
Sidney Harker

Figure 1 **'Gypsy Splendour'**
1939 oil on canvas, Nottingham Castle Museum. By Dame Laura Knight

Contents

Preface

Chapter 1 Who Are The Gypsies?   **1**

       The Buckley Family   3

       Hubert Clee Family   12

       The Varey Family   17

       Lydia Lee   21

       The King Family   24

       The Lee Family   36

       Walter Smith's Family   42

       The Barras Family   50

       Manny Golby   57

       Gypsies at Stow Fair   69

       Gypsies at Appleby Fair   80

       Gypsies in Hollywood, USA   102

       Photographs loaned by Beamish Museum   105

       New Years Day, Lord Mayor's Parade   109

Chapter 2 The Irish Travellers   **116**

Chapter 3 The Scottish Tinkers and Travellers   **127**

Chapter 4 The Gypsies of Epsom Derby   **131**

Chapter 5 Gypsy Fairs and Wagon Painters   **138**

       The Gypsy Wagon Painters   146

Chapter 6 The Travellers   **170**

Chapter 7 Gypsy Living Wagons   **207**

Chapter 8 Not a Big Fat Gypsy Wedding   **221**

Chapter 9 Gypsy Artists   **228**

Acknowledgements   **241**

Figure 2 Walter Smith and Fred Walker

Preface

The Gypsy, The Tinker and The Travelling Man

This is my sixth book I have compiled about Gypsy and Travellers. Not every photograph in this book is of Gypsies. Some of the photographs and information are of the Scottish and Irish Travellers. They were at one time called Tinkers because of their work in metal, usually tin. There are also Romany people who live in Ireland and Scotland.

Other people in this book are neither Gypsies or Travellers, they are people who have either married into Gypsy families or people who most of their lives love the old fashioned way of travelling with horses and wagons, carts and drays - they are indeed a breed apart.

A section of this book is devoted to wagon painters. My last book 'The Gypsy Wagon Painters' was completely devoted to the art of the Gypsy wagon and dray painters. I thought it would be good to include some painters in this book as well.

Another section of the book is about famous artists who were famous for their paintings about Gypsy life. These people include Dame Laura Knight, Sir Alfred Munnings and more up to date artists such as Diana Rosemary Lodge, who is one of the best gypsy painters alive today.

I have included photographs from the London New Year Parade, for the first time ever Gypsy people and a Living Wagon were included (2015).

There is a section on Gypsy weddings (not big fat gypsy weddings) but of the Romany kind.

There are some photographs of the late Sidney Harker in Hollywood U.S.A. with Walter Smith and a Gypsy wagon outside the Warner Brothers Studio.

I do wish to thank all those people who made this book possible, especially Rob Bulmer my son-in-law without whose help I could not have produced this book.

I hope you enjoy reading the comments and information about travelling life and that you will also enjoy looking at the many photographs and paintings.

This may be my last family book in this series but other books will be produced about Gypsy life but in a more condensed form.

John McKale, May 2015

Figure 3 'Northern Gypsies'

Chapter 1

Who Are the Gypsies?

The gypsies are a band of people who have travelled all over Europe, as long as history can remember, but have an ethnic unity and racial originality of which they are justly proud. They can be likened to the Jews, but whereas the Jews have conformed to local law and custom, and have to a certain extent been integrated into the society they live in, the gypsies have always lived on the fringe of society, fiercely defending their right to be free and their natural way of life. In these days many gypsies are now living in houses and permanent caravan sites but still love to maintain their family roots and are not ashamed to be called gypsies.

The origin of the Romanies is by no means clear, but because many similarities between the Romany tongue and Hindustani, there seems little doubt that they originated in India. They travelled from there through the Middle East to Egypt, and this is why they were known as Gypsies. It is thought that while they were in Egypt they picked up their knowledge of palmistry, fortune-telling, and sleight of hand.

It has been suggested that they left India because they were in religious conflict with the Hindus, and this is borne out by their diet. It is thought that they left India between 1000-1200AD, but possibly didn't arrive in Europe for 100 years or so, and did not reach England until the 15th Century. The Romany Gypsies are the oldest ethnic group in Great Britain. The gypsies were known as Gitanos in Spain, Bohemians in France, Zingarie in Italy, Ciganyok in Hungary, and the Dutch called them Heydens meaning heathens. Other countries referred them as Pharoahites. There are gypsies in every major country of the world.

During the 16th Century more and more gypsies poured into Europe as they found life easier than most countries. In some countries such as Spain where the Gitanos were whipped, burnt or branded for a period of 100 years. In England they were deported to America and Jamaica, and as late as Cromwell's time thirteen were hung in Suffolk. Gypsies were branded as thieves and were accused of subtlety, but they were also blamed for the misdeeds of others, and have been persecuted over the years incessantly. It is a little known fact that 400,000 gypsies were sent to the gas chambers under the Nazis. However, they still remain a race apart and are very proud of their Romany blood even today.

Way of Life

Gypsy families roamed the roads in small family groups, usually one wagon on its own, but sometimes two or three would travel together. They had regular stopping places, very often in otherwise little used grassy lanes, and it was here that they would meet up with friends and relations. On stopping, first thing to do was to find for the horse. If grass was plentiful he could graze by the wayside, but if grass was short a suitable field had to found. This had to be spied out before dark, and make sure there were no cattle or horses in the field as it may prove difficult to catch your own, as this had to be done before daylight when the farmer awoke. Likewise, your horse could not be put to graze before dark. This practice was known as 'Pooving the Gry'. Having said that horses were tethered in the fields with ropes or chains, as well as sometimes being hobbled, that is tying the two front lower legs of the horse with a little rope enough for easy movement, but made it difficult for the horse to run away from them.

They did not travel great distances, the New Forest gypsies would not travel much further than Southampton or Salisbury. Those who followed crafts such as pot mending and knife grinding would have a regular route, perhaps calling on the same house twice a year. Local people would put their pots aside to wait for them when they came. The ones that had goods for sale rather than offering a service, such as the basket maker and peg maker, would call more often and would sell to the shops in villages and towns. The larger shops would place a regular order with the gypsies. Some townspeople would not give their knives to gypsies to be sharpened, and would take them to the shops, but little did they know that it was very often the gypsy that sharpened them. Gypsy women would go from door to door selling pegs and flowers made out of wood or paper, this would give the gypsy woman the opportunity to tell fortunes as well.

There were always a lot of gypsies in the New Forest area, because the forest itself was ideally suited to them. There was plenty of grazing for their horses, an abundance of wood for their crafts and fires, a plentiful supply of rabbits and pheasants, and perhaps the odd deer, holly and Christmas trees to be cut and sold, ideal for camping sites, and plenty of horse dealing with the New Forest ponies. Another reason was that there was always a lot of soft fruit grown in the area and this offered employment. One time that gypsies did travel further was hop picking time, and the New Forest gypsies travelled to Kent, because of strawberry picking and when the local harvest was gathered in there was hoeing to be done at that time of the year.

Gypsies left signs in the road for each other, known as the Patrin, usually in the form of an elongated cross made out of twigs, to show which way they had gone.

Figure 4 Gilbert Smith and his wife Mama at Stow Fair, Cotswolds (2013)

The Romany people are still a colourful people although well integrated with the settled population of this country, they still have their own identity they are still proud to be called gypsies. They still love to meet at horse fairs or Christian conventions. Last year I was invited to several gypsy weddings and saw how glad they were to see each other and be among their own kind.

The Buckley Family

Figure 5 Perun and Emily Buckley with the Marco children

Figure 6 The Price family, Doncaster 1954

Figure 7 Buckley family and friends

Figure 8 Creddy Lee with his daughter

Figure 9 The Buckley family

Figure 10 Henrietta Boswell

Figure 11 The Price children

Figure 12 Tony Buckley and
Beng Prince

This wagon was built in 1915 and it is said to be the finest Reading style wagon in existence today.

It was built for a show woman called Tilly Winters who travelled with fairground amusements and I was told by Eileen Buckley that her father who was called Jack Lee once owned it.

The Queen Mother inspected this wagon in the 1960s, while visiting a nearby exhibition for the Royal School of Nursing at Marlborough House. A Miss Willerby had taken the wagon for display at the event. The Queen Mother found the Orton Wagon fascinating, and some say she was given a pair of polished copper and brass water jacks as a gift.

Miss Willerby was an elderly nurse who used to look after gypsy children.

This wagon was also was once owned by John Pockett the wagon painter and restorer. He owned it for over 30 years and it was displayed at Paultons Park.

Figure 23 Her Majesty the Queen Mother

Hubert Clee Family

Figure 24 The Clee family and friends

Figure 25 Hubert Clee and Peter Watton

Figure 26 Hubert and Coraline Clee's grandchildren

Figure 27 Coraline Clee with family member

Figure 28 Clee grandchildren

Figure 29 (Above)
Hubert and Peter

Figure 30 (Right)
Coraline and friend

The Varey Family

Figure 31 Sam Varey

The Gypsy, The Tinker and The Travelling Man

Figure 32 Phil Varey Jr.

Figure 33 Varey family on the road

Figure 34 Varey family arriving at Appleby

Figure 35 Phil Varey with his daughter and Mum

Figure 36 Crystal and Diamond Varey with
Rudy and Robert Dean

Figure 37 Varey family, near Fell End, 2014

Figure 38 Phil Varey Jr. and wife, near Fell End, 2014

Lydia Lee

Lydia Lee, a true Romany legend, was a woman who lived most of her life on the banks of the river Ely beneath Leckwich Hill. At that time the common was speckled with traditionally gaily coloured gypsy wagons. Lydia Lee bore seventeen children in her own van, as well as bringing up five children belonging to one of her five brothers, all of who were killed in the Boer and Great war in 1903.

In 1963 she had to move and ten compassionate businessmen who heard of her plight bought her a new trailer caravan and moved her to a fringe of land near Mardy farm on the Runey shore. She lived there with her disabled son Grainsy. She said, "I never stopped crying for my wagon".

The wagon was burned on the common as they burned her mother's wagon a half century earlier.

Lydia said "A trailer is not a wagon and a car is not a horse".

Lydia died in August 1981.

Figure 39 Lydia Lee

Figure 40 Lydia Lee from Cardiff

Figure 41 Lydia Lee and her sister Dawn

Figure 42 Liddy and Tom Lee

Figure 43 Gypsy wedding, Esther Lee and her granddaughter Sunshine

The King Family (Photographs by Gary Merrit)

Figure 44 Naomi King and her daughter, Stow Fair, 1995

Figure 45 Naomi and John King, Whitechurch, 2001

Figure 46 John King, pheasants, rabbits and sticks

Figure 47 John King gathering holly at Christmas, Whitechurch, 2001

Figure 48 Annie Pockett at Egbury, Hampshire, 1995

Figure 49 John King and daughter fixing the wagon, Arlesford, 1995

Figure 50 John King and family on the road (jalling the drom)

Figure 51 John King and his bender tent, Whitechurch, Hampshire, 1999

Figure 52 Naomi King, Arlesford, Hampshire, 1995
'It was a cold winter'

Figure 53 Naomi James (King)

The Kings' stopping place, 'Atchin Tan', Arlesford, Hampshire, Christmas 1996

Figure 54 (Above)

Figure 55 (Above)

Figure 56 (Left)

Figure 57 The Kings stopping by the wayside

Figure 58 Family around the fire (yog)

Figure 59 Annie's 'Atchin Tan, 1991
Annie Pockett at Whitechurch, Hampshire

Figure 60 Naomi King

Figure 61 Annie Pockett and her son Edward

Figure 62 The King family and friends

Figure 63 John's birthday in their bender tent

Figure 64 Naomi (Omie) King at Bright Walton, 1995

Figure 65 John King

The Lee Family

Figure 66 Kathleen Lee at Appleby New Fair

Figure 67 Fred and Jonas Lee out for a trot

Figure 68 Jonas and Jules Lee with family

Figure 69 Eileen Lee (Kathleen's Mum) and her daughter Pauline

Figure 70 Jim Lee (centre) with his two sons, Jonas and Joseph

Figure 71 Jim Lee

Figure 72 Kathleen and Angeline Lee

Figure 73 Kathleen and Angeline Lee

Figure 74 Fred Lee at caravan site, Birtley

Figure 75 Angeline Lee at the Newcastle upon Tyne Town Moor Fair

Figure 76 The Lee family at Jim's place in Birtley

Figure 77 (Left)
Tina Lee and Grandchildren at
the Fish Quay Festival, North
Shields, Tyneside

Figure 78 (Below)
The Morrison family, North
Shields Fish Quay Festival

Walter Smith's Family

Figure 79 Caroline and Tommy Smith

Figure 80 Sam Price holding his daughter Beryl.
His sister Beryl with her son Nipper and friends

Figure 81 Paddy and Margaret (right), Tommy and Caroline (left)

Figure 82 The Smith family and friends

Figure 83 Tommy and Caroline Smith and family

Figure 84 The Smith family

Figure 85 (Left)
Maureen Price the wife
of Sam Price

Figure 86 (Right)
Sam and Maureen Price
on holiday

Figure 87 The funeral of Creddy Price, the father of Jack Price and grandfather of Sam Price

Figure 88 The funeral of Star Price, wife of Boggie Price

Figure 89 (Left)
Walter and Beryl Smith on their
wedding day

Figure 90 (Right)
Walter and Beryl Smith

Figure 91 Mama, Mary, Beryl, Jaqueline and Dilly Price

Figure 92 Walter Steven Smith and Caesar Burton, 2001
Walter went home to be with the Lord in 2002

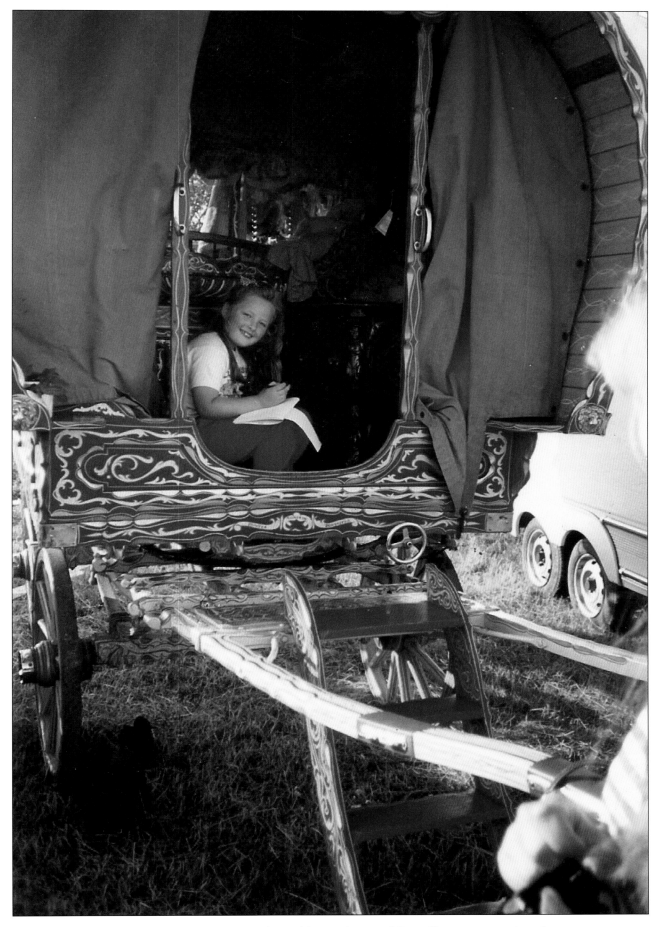

Figure 93 Crystal Savannah Smith, Walter and Beryl's youngest daughter

The Barras Family

Figure 94 Cheeky Nicholson (Berry), Kizzy Berry (Gaskin),
Mudsey Berry (Barras) and Brother Boy Nicholson

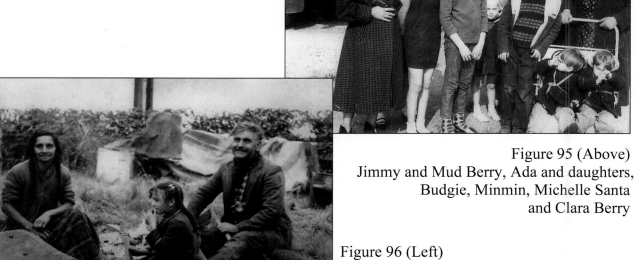

Figure 95 (Above)
Jimmy and Mud Berry, Ada and daughters,
Budgie, Minmin, Michelle Santa
and Clara Berry

Figure 96 (Left)
Jimmy and Clara Berry with granddaughter
Mudsey Nicholson (Barras)

Figure 97 Pat Barras with Sunder the horse

Figure 98 Fred, Pat and Jimmy Barras

Figure 99 Cheeky Berry (Nicholson), daughter of Jimmy Berry the wagon painter

Figure 100 Cheeky Nicholson (Berry) with baby Mudsey

Figure 101 Fred and Pat Barras

Figure 102 Fred Barras at Lee Gap Fair, Wakefield

Figure 103 Joseph Walter, Margaret Ann Walter,
Prudence Barras and Mary Faith Walter

Figure 104 Tom and Prudence Barras

Figure 105 The Barras and Wiltshire families

Figure 106 Mudsey Barras

Figure 107 Left to right, Jimmy Barras with baby Jimmy, Alex, Mudsey and
Door Knocker (the horse)

Figure 108 Jimmy Berry and wife Clara with granddaughter Mudsey Nicholson (Barras)

Figure 109 Alex and Mudsey's wedding day.
Jimmy and Clara (Mud) Berry with Fred and Pat Barras

Figure 110 Fred Barras

Figure 111 Mudsey Barras with oldest boy
Jimmy, daughter Chanel and baby son Alex

Figure 112 Chanel, Alex, Jimmy
and Mudsey Barras

Manny Golby, DCM

'The Fighting Man of the Fruit Country'

The area of Swanick and Hedge End Southampton was a major fruit growing area particularly for strawberries; it had a direct link to the London markets. Many gypsies travelled to this area for work and many decedents of these families still live in and around Southampton today. This area of Southampton was known as 'the fruit county'

Manny was at work in a strawberry field when the military police came to take him for the army and he was taken to the Hampshire regiment. After basic training he was sent home to marry his wife Charlotte legally as it was likely he would be killed in the First World war, his wife would then get a pension from the army. Manny was transferred from the Hampshire regiment to the Duke of Cornwall's light infantry in 1915 (see picture).

From there, he was sent overseas to Gibraltar where later in life, he told his son (Manny Golby Jnr) that he came '32nd in a race to the top of the rock in Gibraltar', his son Manny said '32nd is not much good', to which his father replied 'it was out of 8000'.

From Gibraltar he was sent to Egypt to train to fight the Turks, while in Egypt he became champion of 'All His Majesties Services' for boxing (see Figure 114 with cup). He was transferred to Devonshire regiment and made a company runner. His job was to run between the lines carrying messages (as there were no radios or

Figure 113 Picture taken while Manny was in the Duke of Cornwall Light Infantry, PTE 33433 Golby, June 1916

mobile phones then). He was chosen because he was a good athlete, also being a gypsy he had no formal education and could not read or write, so if captured he could not reveal what was in the message. While returning with messages he was asked to guide wounded soldiers back to the lines. He noticed one man lagging behind who was awkward and noisy. Manny said 'I grabbed him by the hair' and then in a loud whisper said 'you will get us all killed'. The soldier replied 'I'm sorry I'm blind'. Manny then tied the soldier to himself and crawled back with the man on his back. For this Manny was 'MENTIONED IN DISPATCHES' (the oak tree medals).

While in Italy he was sighted for the Distinguished Conduct Medal for conspicuous gallantry as company runner (see Figure 117 London Gazette cutting). Manny was finally transferred to the Manchester regiment, also serving in Italy in the Piave, again as company runner.

Figure 114 Picture taken in Egypt when Manny was Champion of all His Majesties Services

Company runners were usually sent out in different directions usually two men with the same message, most were killed.

After the First World War Manny settled back in Swanick on a piece of ground he called Sunny Devon. Manny was only a private soldier but was visited regularly by a Captain Ware (later Major Ware) from the Bridport area of Somerset. They would go to the wood shed and drink together and talk about the war, it was said that Manny had saved the Captains life and may explain why he visited a Gypsy a world away from his life, as he was part of the landed gentry. If anyone from Major Wares family could fill in the blanks, we would love to know the full story. Major Ware continued to visit until his death in the 1960s. When Manny returned from the war he was known as Manny Golby who won the medal or THE FIGHTING MAN OF THE FRUIT COUNTRY.

Manny had six children, Charity, Caroline, Albert, Sissy, Mary, and Manny Jnr (Albert fought in Italy in the Second World War, a coincidence that both father and son both fought for their country in Italy in two world wars).

Manny made his living from making fencing stakes which they sold at Salisbury market and also buying and selling scrap metal. He used to drive from Southampton to the New Forest where Gypsies lived in the 'compounds'. He would buy metal, jam jars and bottles as well as rags. The Gypsies from the 'compounds' would collect the metal on carts and horses. Manny having a lorry was able to cover greater distances and get a better price for the metal because of the quantity and selling in the city of Southampton ,where metal is still exported from today.

Figure 115 Left to Right, Standing farm worker, Manny Golby, Mary and Sissy. Seated Manny and Charlotte.
1947 in the hop fields

In winter time Manny and his sons went to Somerset and cut mistletoe out of the apple trees, tied it in cloth or lorry sheets and sent it back on the train to Swanick, they would bring Christmas trees back home on the lorry.

Manny's great grandchildren, pictured over the page have just had their first fights in amateur boxing, hopefully they will keep up this sport in the future.

Figure 116 The Golby family

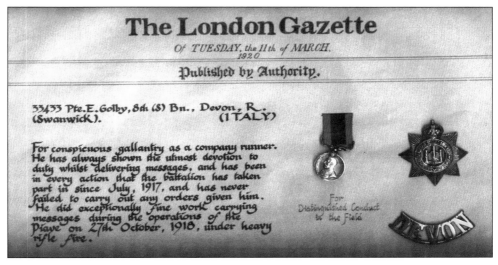

Figure 117 (Above)
London Gazette

Figure 118 (Left)
Manny's medals

Figure 119 The grave of Emanuel and Charlotte Golby

Pte. E. Golby
Born 1894 Died 1970
1915 enlisted in the Hampshire Regiment for basic training.

1916 (May) transferred to The Duke of Conwalls light infantry 3rd battalion serial number 27380.

1917(February) sent overseas to Egypt via Aden, Boxing Champion All His Majesty's Services Egypt.

1918 (30th May) 8th battalion of the Devon Regiment serial number 33433 (company runner) in Italy Mentioned in Despatches.

1918(27th October) serial number 33433 8th Devon Regiment Company runner awarded The Distinguished Conduct Medal for 'Conspicuous Gallantry under heavy rifle fire' Piave Italy.

1918 (1st November) 22nd battalion Manchester Regiment serial number 88405 Piave and Vittoria-Veneto.

1919 returned home awarded The War Medal and The Victory Medal serial number 88405 Pte E. Golby 22nd battalion of The Manchester Regiment.

Figure 120 Manny's army history

Figure 121
Lewis and Mitchell, two of Manny's great grandchildren

Further photographs of the Gypsy community

Figure 122 Gordon Boswell and family

Figure 123 Group of travellers including Billy Welsh and Sidney Harker at Appleby New Fair

Figure 124 Charmaine Mitchell at Fell End, Cumbria, 2012

Figure 125 Charmaine Mitchell with her son Luke

Figure 126 The Mitchell family camped near Fell End, Cumbria, 2012

Figure 127 Robert and Ada Farrow camping near Hawes, 2014

Figure 128 Duran Coulson at Appleby Fair, 2014

Figure 129 Kathleen Lee (Scagga's wife), Appleby Fair in the 1970s

Figure 130 Scagga Lee at Appleby with grandson John and a friend

Figure 131 Gypsies at Stow Fair

Figure 132 Edna Elliot and Eileen Rawlings

Gypsies at Stow Fair

Figure 133 Sid Biddle, Stow Fair, 2013

Figure 134 Snowy Gentle, Stow Fair, 2013

Figure 135 A wet day at Stow Fair, 2013

Figure 136

Figure 137 Stow Fair

Figure 138 Boy with horses at Stow Fair

Figure 139 Jonny McKale (John's son) helping his Dad to sell books,
Stow Fair, 2013

Figure 140 (Left)
Ted Sykes and brother
Boy Nicholson, Stow
Fair, 2013

Figure 141 (Right)
Stow Fair, 2013

Figure 142
John Finney at Stow Fair

Figure 143 John and Linda Finney, Stow Fair

Figure 144 Gypsy men

Figure 145 Walter Smith and his brothers at Stow Fair

Figure 146 Stow Fair

Figure 147 Mick Darling at Stow Fair

Gypsies at Appleby Fair

Figure 148 Appleby Fair, 1970s

Figure 149 Appleby Fair, 1970s

Figure 150 Having a deal at Appleby Fair, 1970s

Figure 151 The Flashing Lane at Appleby Fair, 1970s

Figure 152 Appleby, 1970s

Figure 153 Appleby Fair

Figure 154 Isla St Clair buying a horse at Appleby Fair, 1980s

Figure 155 (Left)

Figure 156 (Below)

Figure 157 (Above)

Figure 158 (Right)

Figure 159 A wagon pulled by four horses (something different), 2014

Figure 160 (Above)

Figure 161 (Left)

Figure 162 Gypsies at Appleby Fair

Figure 163 Gypsies at Appleby Fair

Figure 164 Appleby Fair

Figure 165 Appleby Fair

Figure 166 Gypsy men at Appleby

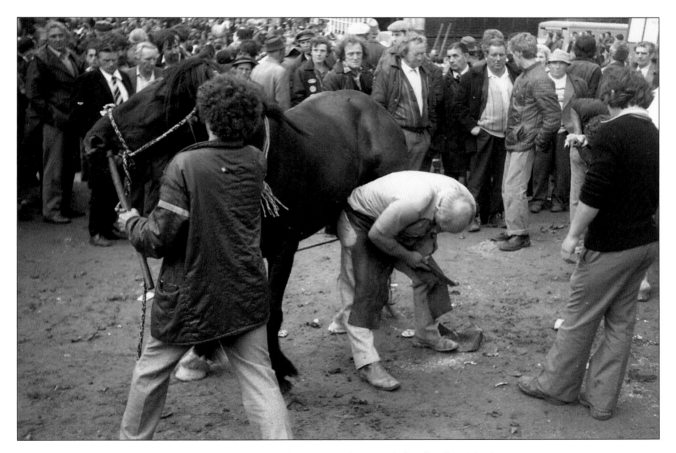

Figure 167 A farrier at work, Appleby in the 1970s

Figure 168 (Above)
Putting a metal rim on
a wheel

Figure 169 (Right)

Figure 170

Figure 171

Figure 172

Figure 173

Figure 174 Reading auction

Figure 175 Gypsy Christian convention

Figure 176 Towson Nicholson, 1960s

Figure 177 Joe Thompson (Barras)

Figure 178 Yarm Fair near Stockton on Tees, early 1920s

Figure 179 (Above)

Figure 180 (Right)

Figure 181 (Left)

Figure 182 (Above)

Figure 183 (Above)

Figure 184 (Right)

Figure 185 Appleby Fair

Figure 186 Westmorland Star trailer caravan at Appleby Fair

Figure 187 (Left)
Lewis Boswell at
Appleby

Figure 188 (Below)
Appleby Fair

Figure 189 Rose-Anne and John Boy Hayden's wedding at the Gypsy Church Darlington

Figure 190 Angeline Lee, John McKale with Blackie and Tina Lee at John
Boy and Rose-Anne Hayden's wedding

Figure 191 Connie and Liam Smith at the Town Moor Hoppings,
Newcastle upon Tyne

Figure 192 Maureen Sowerby with Donny Boswell and Lias Wharton, at Branthwaites Gift Shop, Appleby

Gypsies in Hollywood, USA

Figure 193 Walter Smith and Sid Harker in Hollywood

Figure 194

Figure 195 Outside Warner Brothers' film studio

Figure 196

Figure 197

Photographs loaned from Beamish Museum

Figure 198 (Above)

Figure 199 (Right)
Appleby Fair in
the 1930s

Figure 200 (Above)

Figure 201 (Right)

Figure 202 (Above)

Figure 203 (Right)

Figure 204 (Above)
Joe Nicholson
bringing his
wagon to Beamish
Museum

Figure 205 (Right)

New Years Day Lord Mayor's Parade, London, 2015

London's New Year's Day Parade has developed into one of the world's greatest street spectaculars with up to 10,000 performers from across continents, hundreds of thousands of spectators, and a 'live' TV audience of several hundred million.

There are many floats, lots of marching bands and many horse drawn carriages. This year, for the first time ever, there was a representation from the Gypsy and Traveller community. This was organised by Greg Yates (Clearwater Gypsies).

I am sure you will be pleased to see a Gypsy living wagon pulled by a white horse and Romany people take part in this spectacular event. The event starts at the Ritz Hotel in Piccadilly and goes through the city of Westminster winding its way past Buckingham Palace. I am sure the Gypsy community will be very proud to see that they were represented with such a lovely turnout of wagons, horses and Gypsy people.

Figure 206 (Above)

Figure 207 (Right)

Figure 208 Jim Cannon

Figure 209 Cannon family

Figure 210 (Above)
Greg Yates with Jim and
Joey Cannon

Figure 211 (Above)
Greg Yates and the
Cannon family

Figure 212 (Left)
The Cannon family

Figure 213 The Cannon family

Figure 214 Buckingham Palace in the background. A very good turnout.

Figure 215 Caroline Marsh. Caroline is the organiser of the parade

Figure 216 Right Greg Yates, left Joey Cannon, with the rest of the family in the wagon

Figure 217 Cannon family with Edwin (Cappy) Young

Figure 218 Cannon family enjoying the parade

Figure 219

Figure 220 Cannon family

Chapter 2

The Irish Travellers

Irish travellers are also called Pavee, Tinkers, or Gypsies. They are a traditionally itinerant ethnic group who maintain a set of traditions. Although these people are predominantly English speaking some use an old traveller's language called Shelta and other similar cants or a language called Gammon. It is said that ten percent of the Gammon language comes from Romany. It is said that there are 6000 people in Ireland who still use this language, but having said that statistically there are 86,000 Irish Travellers worldwide.

Between 1845 to 1860, about 2,500 Irish Travellers moved to the U.S.A because of the potato famine. There is a town in South Carolina just outside Augusta called Murphy Village and is made up of Irish Travelling people.

The travellers refer themselves as Minkiers or Pavees, which literally means walking people. Sometimes they are also known as Knackers or Tinkers (or tinsmiths) the meaning of Tinkers is because they mend tin ware such as pots and pans and knackers being the acquisition of taking dead or old horses to the slaughter. Today their occupation is mainly road mending, tree loping, roofing, and collecting scrap metal and rags.

There are a large percentage of Travellers living in Britain, something like 15,000 if we include them with the Romanys there must be something like 300,000 travellers in the U.K. The Romany people and the Irish Travellers don't mix very well, but there has been some inter marriage among the two groups.

Figure 221

Figure 222 (Above)

Figure 223 (Above)

Figure 224 (Above)

Figure 225 (Left)

Puck Fair, Killorglin, County Kerry, Ireland

Ireland's Oldest Fair

One of Ireland's oldest and continuously run fairs has now moved to a very large field walking distance from the town. Originally this fair took place on the streets of the town of Killorglin. Buying / selling of horses, ponies, donkeys and equipment, start early in the morning and go on continuously throughout the day, the fair runs from the 10th - 12th of August each year.

History

The most widely mentioned story relating to the origin of King Puck, associates him with the English Ironside leader Oliver Cromwell. It is related that while the "Roundheads" were pillaging the countryside around Shanara and Kilgobnet at the foot of the McGillycuddy Reeks, they routed a herd of goats grazing on the upland. The animals took flight before the raiders, and the he-goat or "Puck" broke away on his own and lost contact with the herd. While the others headed for the mountains he went towards Cill Orglain (Killorglin) on the banks of the river Laune. His arrival there in a state of semi exhaustion alerted the inhabitants of the approaching danger and they immediately set about protecting themselves and their stock.

It is said that in recognition of the service rendered by the goat, the people decided to institute a special festival in his honour and this festival has been held ever since.

Other legends regarding the origin of "King Puck" relates to the time of Daniel O'Connell, who in 1808 was an unknown barrister. It seems that before that year, the August Fair held in Killorglin had been a toll fair, but an act of British Parliament empowered the Viceroy or Lord Lieutenant in Dublin to make an order, at his own discretion, making it unlawful to levy tolls on cattle, horses or sheep fairs. Tolls in Killorglin at this time were collected by the local landlord – Mr Blennerhassett, who had fallen into bad graces with the authorities in Dublin Castle and as a result the Viceroy robbed him of the right to levy tolls. Blennerhassett enlisted the services of the young Daniel O'Connell, who in an effort to reverse the decision decided that goats were not covered by the document and that the landlord would be legally entitled to hold a goat fair and levy tolls as usual.

Thus the fair was promptly advertised as taking place on August 10th 1808 and on that day a goat was hoisted on a stage to show all attending that the fair was indeed a goat fair, thus Blennerhassett collected the money and Killorglin gained a King.

Whatever its origins, the fair has long been and continues to be the main social, economic and cultural event in the Killorglin calendar. It is a time when old friends meet, when new friendships are forged and the cares of everyday living are put on hold.

Killorglin celebrated the anniversary of over 400 years of the first recorded "Puck Fair". In 1613 King James 1st mentioned the fair in a Charter to be granted to landlord Jenkins Conway.

Over many years "Puck Fair" has also been the meeting place of the Gypsies and Irish Tinkers. One person said "People watching is part of the Puck Fair". Gypsy women were seen wearing long skirts and dangling earrings and were an amazing sight. Horse dealing is also done and local farmers bring their livestock to be seen and sold. There is also horse trotting among the travelling community and also a large fun fair. The streets are full of people who are there to be part of the yearly meeting.

The fair usually lasts for three days and it's a time when friends meet as they do at the famous Appleby Fair in Cumbria, England.

Figure 226
If you miss the August Puck Fair, you can still see a representation of King
Puck. A bronze statue of the Billy Goat stands next to Killorglin's River
Laune at the bridge end of the main street.

Puck Fair pictures probably in the 1950s and 1960s

Figure 227 Puck Fair

Figure 228 Puck Fair

Figure 229 Puck Fair

Figure 230 Puck Fair

Figure 231 Puck Fair

Figure 232 Puck Fair

Figure 233 Puck Fair, looks like the 1960s

Figure 234 Puck Fair

Ballinasloe Horse Fair, County Galway, Ireland

The Ballinasloe horse fair is held annually at the town of Ballinasloe which is the second largest town in County Galway, in the West of Ireland. It is one of Europe's oldest and largest horse fairs, dating back to the 18th century. This annual event attracts 100,000 visitors from all over the world, many returning to the town each year. The town is also renowned for horse and pony riding, show jumping and other equestrian activities which take place during the year.

The fair lasts nine days and starts the first Saturday in October, when a parade through the town takes place.

There is a 6 acre field called "fair green" where horses are sold, trotted and flashed.

The fair is known by a variety of names, including the "Ballinasloe October Fair" and the "Great Fair". At one stage Ballinasloe Fair was the largest horse fair in Europe.

Association with the Travelling Community

The Ballinasloe Horse Fair has a long traditional association with the Irish travelling community who regularly congregate at the fair. Ballinasloe ranks with the Appleby Horse Fair in Appleby-in-Westmorland in importance for this community.

Figure 235 Ballinasloe Fair

Figure 236 Ballinasloe Fair

Figure 237 Ballinasloe Fair

Figure 238 Flashing horses

Figure 239 Flashing horses

Chapter 3

The Scottish Tinkers and Travellers

There are more than a half dozen types of travelling people in Scotland, speaking a variety of different languages and retaining a variety of distinct customs, histories and traditions. These groups include Highland Scottish Travellers, Lowland Scottish Travellers and Romany Gypsies.

Highland Scottish Travellers, while perhaps one of Europe's last nomadic people, are not Romany people. They are distinct from them ethnically, culturally and linguistically. They are indigenous Gaelic speaking people. In Scottish Gaelic they are known as Ceardannan or ("craftsmen").

The word tinker itself comes from the Gaelic "tinceard" or tinsmith. Poetically known as the Summer Walkers they are also known or referred to as traivellers, traivelling fowk and nawkers. These people carry clan names like Macfie, Stewart, MacDonald, Cameron, Williamson and Macmillan. They would pitch their bender or rod tents at the edge of a village and earn money as tinsmiths, hawkers, horse dealers or pearl fishermen. They would also earn money as farm workers picking berries and also entertain the country folk.

It is estimated that only 2,000 Scottish Travellers continue to lead their traditional lifestyle on the roads. Many of them now live on caravan sites for travellers and not a few live in houses. These folks are not ashamed to be identified as travellers. They are still fiercely discriminated against today and those familiar with the travellers detect an underlying serge of persecution and despair amongst these people who cherish the traditional ways of their fore fathers.

Figure 240

Figure 241
A tinker woman or traveller with tin-ware at Glenelg.
Isobella MacDonald was the wife of a travelling tinsmith, with her son on her back and her sister
Harriet Stewart, aged nine. Photograph by Bob Charnley

Figure 242 Scottish Tinkers

Figure 243 Scottish Tinkers

Figure 244

Figure 245

Chapter 4

The Gypsies at the Epsom Derby, Surrey

The Derby has been run at Epsom since **1779** except in all the years during the World Wars, from **1915** to **1918** and **1940** to **1945** it was run at Newmarket.

EPSOM FAIR

For many years the Derby was run on a Wednesday or a Thursday and on those days huge crowds would come from London, not only to see the races but to enjoy the entertainment too.

In the **1850s** Charles Dickens visited Epsom Downs to view the races. Entertainers such as clowns, musicians and conjurers plied their trade and entertained the crowds of people.

In the **1880s** the steam driven fairground rides were introduced and the fair lasted for ten days and catered for hundreds and thousands of people. Later on as the number of people dwindled the length of the fair was reduced to three or four days and in **2009** the fairground was closed to make room for car parking.

Gypsies and Travellers have been going to Epsom Derby for hundreds of years, but last year (2014) the annual gypsy holiday on the Downs featured a mere thirty metre enclosure which showed the best of traditional and modern gypsy culture.

Some interesting statistics.

1769. The first mention of gypsies on Epsom Downs.

1820. Jack Cooper, a gypsy prize fighter from Windsor, takes on West Country Dick at the Derby and knocks him out after 29 rounds.

1830. Fortune telling becomes profitable. The gypsy woman, with the flashing yellow and red handkerchief about her head, and the strange silvery-hoarse voice works the crowd, often carrying a baby with her while the children mind the tent.

1863. The first evidence for wagons at the Derby. At first these are simple tilt carts with tarpaulin roof, but within twenty years expensive Reading and Burton wagons appear on the Downs. Many families continue to live in benders, not so interesting to artists!

1874. Epsom has become a major Romani centre, under the name of **Boro Nashimescro Tan** – 'the place with the big racecourse'. Evangelists from London book a tent and give gospel addresses to 120 gypsies, who listen politely and eat a large tea.

1928. The Derby becomes a magnet for artists. Alfred Munnings accompanies Gregorys, Lovedays and Lees from Binstead; Laura Knight meets the Smiths from Iver. Their portraits show men and women dressed at their best beside elaborately carved living wagons.

1967. A thousand gypsy families assembled each year for the Derby, according to estimates from the gypsy council.

1971. Agreement is reached with the Conservators with an authorised gypsy site set up to the west of the Grandstand. Fortune telling is still carried on by the granddaughters or great granddaughters of Gypsy Lee and others but the Derby is increasingly a gypsy holiday.

The Appleby Fair in Cumbria is on at the same time or pretty close and is probably more popular to the gypsies than any where else.

Figure 246
'The Derby Day' by William Powell Frith 1819 - 1909,
oil on canvas, Tate Britain, London

Figure 247 The Lee family at Epsom in the 1960s

Figure 248 Tommy Gaskin pulling on to the Derby

Figure 249 'Manging lova from the Gorja Rawnies'

Figure 250 Gypsy women selling flowers to the aristocracy at Epsom

Figure 251 Gypsies at Epsom Downs, 1920s

Figure 252 Gypsies at Epsom Races

Figure 253 Famous tipster, Prince Monolulu

Figure 254 Gypsies at Epsom Races

Figure 255 Gypsies at Epsom Downs

Figure 256 Gypsies at Epsom Downs

Chapter 5

Gypsy Fairs and Wagon Painters

Gypsy horse fairs are not as many as they used to be, but having said that there are still many old and new fairs held each year in Britain. The most popular horse fair is **Appleby in Westmorland** now (Cumbria) where thousands of Gypsies and Travellers from all over the world assemble.

Figure 257

Figure 258

Stow Fair

Stow Fair in the Cotswolds (Stow-on-the-Wold), Gloucestershire is held twice a year in the Spring and in the Autumn, this fair is only for one day and is held two minutes walk from the town centre.

Figure 259 Mr and Mrs Elliot at Stow Fair

Figure 260 Travellers at Stow Fair

Lee Gap Fair

Lee Gap fair is said to be the oldest fair and is held twice a year, for one day only. The second fair is called Latter Lee this is a nice little fair and a good day out. It has a market with horses, carts and wagons, horse tack and car boot stuff usually for sale.

Figure 261 (Above)
Mick and Susy Darling at Lee
Gap Fair

Figure 262 (Above)
Gypsy market

Figure 263 (Left)
Horses for sale

Seamer Fair

Seamer Fair near Scarborough has had a revival and is now attended by many hundreds of people. It is a good fair and very interesting with lots of personalities from the Gypsy and traveller world in attendance. Horses are flashed, wagons, drays, carts are for sale and there is a good market with lots of things to tempt those looking for a bargain.

Figure 264 The Sykes family

Figure 265 Horses for sale

Yarm Fair

Yarm Fair near Stockton-on-Tees is a very old fair and is mainly run by the Showmen's Guild. One part of the busy town is a large fun fair and at the other end there are the gypsies and travellers. Horses are still sold and on the Saturday of the fair the horses are flashed up and down the road. The traffic is stopped from entering the town on that morning. The fair is opened by the Lord Mayor and other important council officers.

Figure 266

Figure 267 Woods, Mansons and Locks at Yarm Fair

Kenilworth Fair

There are lots of other fairs held in the country, **Kenilworth Fair** Warwickshire is becoming very popular and is a very nice fair. I believe this is held on a Sunday three or four times a year. There is lots to see, horses are for sale and there is a huge market which lots of Gypsy and traveller people attend.

Figure 268 (Above)
Zacc Finney and son at
Kenilworth fair

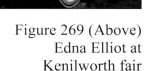

Figure 269 (Above)
Edna Elliot at
Kenilworth fair

Figure 270 (Left)
Gypsy market

Barnet Fair

Barnet Fair near London is still held every year and is worth a visit, although not as big as it once was it is still a much loved fair and needs your support.

Figure 271 (Above)
Boswell brothers with Dave
Peacock (centre). Dave is an
entertainer in the
Chas & Dave band

Figure 272 (Above)
Flashing the horses

Figure 273 (Right)
Dray for sale, painted by
Tom Stephenson

St. Boswell's Fair

St. Boswell's Fair in the Scottish Borders is a fair that also needs your support. It was once a thriving horse fair but now needs more gypsies and travellers to spend a few days there. Last year there was a very good exhibition held in the Civic Hall and hundreds of the travelling community attended.

There are lots of photographs in this book and my other books of horse fairs. I have not mentioned all of the fairs that are held each year, but they are advertised in the Travellers Times magazine.

Figure 274 Blackie Lee with his grandson Brandon and John Baxter

Figure 275 On the green at St. Boswell's Fair, Scottish Borders

The Gypsy Wagon Painters

Gypsy living wagons were elaborately decorated, hand carved and ornately painted with traditional Romany symbols. Gypsies would participate in the ornate carving and decoration, being skilled woodcarvers themselves, but would leave the main construction to a professional specialised coach builder. Examples of famous wagon artists responsible for early development of gypsy wagon art are the late Jimmy Berry, Tom Stephenson, Tom Gaskin and Joe Barras (Thompson) and Peter Ingram. Modern contemporary decorators continuing to shape this colourful tradition include artists such as John Pockett, John Greenwood ('Yorkie'), Lol Thompson and many others.

Much of the wealth of the Gypsy living wagon is displayed in the number of carvings, paintings and vine-work, including elaborate scroll working. Paintings incorporate aspects of the Romany lifestyle, including horses, birds, dogs and floral designs. Scroll working is heightened by the use of between 10 to 100, or even more, books of gold leaf applied as decoration to a living wagon. Each painter was identified by their own method of design.

A traditional Gypsy wagon is pulled by one or two plodding horses and there are six different types of wagons.

The modern Romany travellers in the 1920s proudly clung to their decorative wagons, although the economics of their way of life was in upheaval due to the horse trading industry. In this present day Gypsies are more likely to live in trailer

Figure 276 John (Yorkie) Greenwood

caravans. In the 1960s there was a great decline in the use of horse drawn living wagons. One man told me that at the Appleby Horse Fair in the late '60s he counted only six Bow Topped wagons. Since then there has been a revival of the gypsy wagons and many are being restored and built by reputable builders such as Jowetts and other firms.

Jimmy Berry

Figure 277

Figure 278

Tommy Gaskin

Tommy Gaskin was from the North of England and lived most of his life in the Doncaster area. Tommy was noted to be one of the best remembered wagon painters in the country. He had numerous other abilities, one of which was sign writing.

Figure 279 Tommy Gaskin's Bill Wrights wagon at the Lee Gap Fair, 1965

Figure 280 Tommy and Lucy Gaskin camping overnight in Leeds, 1930s

Tom Stephenson

Figure 281 Tom Stephenson

Figure 282 Excellent workmanship

John Pickett

John Hugh William Pickett was born in Salisbury on 19th March 1950, the youngest child and only son of Ralph and Barbara Pickett of Tisbury. On leaving school at sixteen John went to Swindon Art College, he had met many travellers by this time, through his father and had built his first Gypsy wagon at the age of fourteen. John's reputation grew. By the 1980s everyone knew that he was the best and the work came piling in. He built wagons for Anthony Sampson (author of *The Scholar Gypsy* and many other works), for the folk duo Chas and Dave, who remain lifelong friends and for the entrepreneur Sean Martin.

Figure 283 (Above)

Figure 284 (Left)

Figure 285 Henry and George Gaskin with Charlotte Smith, 1978, being
interviewed by Southern Television

Joe Thompson (Barras)

Joe Thompson is a well known wagon builder and painter of horse drawn vehicles. Joe is a man now in his early 70s. Joe said he last painted a Gypsy wagon in the 1970s. In those days he was at the top of his league as a Gypsy wagon builder, cart builder and painter. Since then he has been involved in the making of horse drawn carriages and has a saddlery business. His family were, and are, part of the Gypsy and Traveller fraternity.

Figure 286 Tom Barras, Jimmy Berry and Joe Thompson (Barras)

Figure 287 Henry and Winney Randell with a wagon made by Joe Thompson

Figure 288
Henry and Winney Randell from Norfolk. This wagon was built and painted
by Joe Thompson (Barras), Thinford, near Bishop Auckland, Co. Durham.

John (Yorkie) Greenwood

Figure 289 John (Yorkie) Greenwood.
Yorkie is noted as probably the best wagon painter in the country

Figure 290 Yorkie and his son John.
Yorkie is one of the finest wagon painters in the country

Figure 291 (Above)
Yorkie with newly painted
Charlotte Smith's wagon

Figure 292 (Right)
John (Yorkie) Greenwood

John Pockett

John Pockett, wagon painter and restorer, one of the finest craftsmen in the country.

Figure 293 (Above)
Street roundabout painted and
restored by John Pockett

Figure 294 (Left)
John Pockett

Lol Thompson

Lawrence (Lol) Thompson is one of the most well known and respected wagon painters in the North of England. His workmanship is of a high standard and also is in much demand. Lol sometimes paints cars and lorries for people, he said he could paint a motor in a day, but it takes weeks to paint a wagon from top to bottom; 'that's provided you're in shelter, because if you're outside you have to wait a few days for the paint to dry because of the dew.'

Figure 295

Dave Peacock

Dave Peacock is better known as one half of the rock group Chas & Dave. He gives much of his time to restoring and painting Gypsy caravans. Dave said Gypsy wagons are in his blood as his grandparents were travellers and he has not forgotten his Gypsy roots. Dave trained as a sign writer when he left school and got into painting wagons and London trolleys.

Figure 296 Jimmy Berry with Dave Peacock. Dave is an excellent wagon painter and stems from a Gypsy family

Figure 297 Wagon built and painted by Dave Peacock

Ian Stanton, Ryton, Tyneside

Ian Stanton has been painting living wagons, drays, rollies and carts since he was a young man. Although he has a scrap metal business his main time is given over to painting. Ian who is now in his early sixties has painted hundreds of horse drawn vehicles. Ian is a very good scroller and gilder and has produced over the years some very good work to a good standard. Some of his work is as good as you can get anywhere. He also is a good sign writer. Ian learned some of his skills from the late Norman Ramshaw. The two men worked together for many years until the recent sad death of Norman. Ian now works alone and is still enjoying the love of his life which is painting. I often see Ian and we have long chats together and I have admired his skills in wagon painting.

Figure 298

Figure 299 (Above)

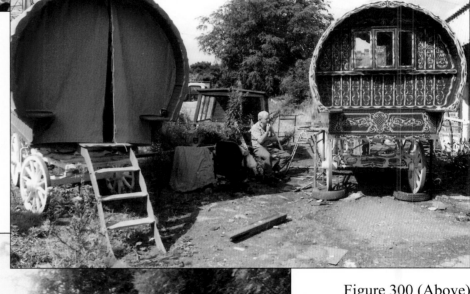

Figure 300 (Above)

Figure 301 (Left)

Figure 302 Ian Stanton

Graham Blowman

Figure 303 (Above)

Figure 304 (Right)

Norman Ramshaw, Ryton on Tyne

Norman was an excellent painter of fruit and horse heads and this example of his work was painted on the back board of a dray. Norman sadly passed away about two years ago.

Figure 305

Figure 306 Cart built and painted by Norman

James Burnside, County Durham

James is a fine up and coming young painter and his work is of excellent quality for his age.

Figure 307

Figure 308

Joe Davidson, Blackpool

Joe is a top class wagon builder and wheel right, he along side his wife do a very good paint job.

Figure 309

James Brindley

Figure 310

Figure 311

Billy Joe Hall, Yorkshire

Billy Joe is an excellent wagon painter, a young man with great ability.

Figure 312

Figure 313

Figure 314 An example of Billy Joe's excellent recent work

Figure 315 Billy Joe and Savannah on their wedding day

Chapter 6

The Travellers

There is a large group, that cover a wide variety of people, who are not Gypsies or Irish or Scottish Travellers, they are people who over the years have associated themselves with both. These people love the travelling way of life and you will find them at most Gypsy horse fairs and drives. They love horses and living wagons and many of them posses both. A lot of these people have kept alive the old Gypsy way of life, when most Gypsies live in modern trailer caravans settled on council caravan sites or live in houses, these people help to preserve the old way of Gypsy life.

In this chapter I have tried to include them because they play a big part of the Gypsy and traveller culture. Some of these people have married into Romany families although having said that the Romany people don't like to marry out of their own race.

Richie Graham

Richie Graham lives in Sacriston, Co. Durham. Although he and his family are not Gypsies they are certainly travellers. Richie grew up surrounded by Gypsy life and has a great knowledge about Gypsies, living wagons, horses, and he is also a very good wagon painter. His hobby is making miniature wagons and carts. He is also an excellent stool and money box maker. The following photographs are of his family and friends.

Figure 316 (Above)
Brett Graham

Figure 317 (Right)
Brett Graham

Figure 318 Brett Graham

Figure 319 Brett Graham

Figure 320 Alan Graham

Figure 321 Alan Graham

Figure 323 (Below)
Alan Graham

Figure 322 (Above)
The Graham family

Figure 324 (Left)
Billy Gentle, Dick Hope, Alan Graham
and Kevin Hope

Figure 325
Kevin Hope on Newcastle Town Moor Fair, 2014

Joe Carr, North Yorkshire

Figure 326 (Left)
Joe Carr and friend

Figure 327 (Right)
Joe Carr

Figure 328

Figure 329

Figure 330
John Greenwood (Yorkie) with a horse called Dan, bred by Joe Thompson.
Linewood cart built by Jowetts

Figure 331
James Burnside (wagon painter)

Figure 332 (Left)

Figure 333

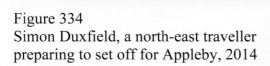

Figure 334
Simon Duxfield, a north-east traveller
preparing to set off for Appleby, 2014

Figure 335 (Right)

Figure 336

Figure 337 Two very old photographs of traveller life (Beamish Museum)

Figure 338 Billy Joe Hall's Great Grandfather with a street roundabout

Figure 339 Billy Joe Hall's Great Grandfather with a street roundabout

Figure 340 Jonny and Sheila Francis at Lee Gap fair, 2014

Figure 341 Travellers at Lee Gap Fair, 2014

Figure 342 Joe Davidson at Lee Gap Fair, 2014

Figure 343 Malcolm Blenkinsop with Toney and Lillian Peart at Melmerby, Cumbria, waiting to pull onto Appleby, 2014

Figure 344 Malcolm and Liam Blenkinsop at Melmerby

Figure 345 Travellers at Fell End, near Kirkby Stephen

Figure 346 Travellers at Stow Fair, 2014

Figure 347 Wagons belonging to the Walker family

Figure 348 Wagons at Fell End, Cumbria

Figure 349 Gypsy camp near Fell End, Cumbria

Figure 350 Jowett Brothers wagon and advertisement

Philip and David Jowett are probably amongst the best wagon builders in the country. Their sons were at Fell End heading towards Appleby for the 2014 fair.

Figure 351

Figure 352 Girl on horse near Fell End, Cumbria, waiting to pull onto
Appleby Fair, 2014

Figure 353 Christian meeting at Stow Fair

Figure 354 Christian meeting at Stow Fair

Figure 355 Travellers pulling onto Appleby

Figure 356 Lorry and dray, Fell End

Figure 357 Wagons for sale

Figure 358 From Belfast to Appleby

Figure 359 (Above)

Figure 360 (Above)
Shoeing horses at Fell End

Figure 361 (Left)

Figure 362 Appleby Fair

Figure 363 Appleby Fair

Figure 364 (Above)
Leaving Fell End for Appleby

Figure 365 (Right)
Appleby Fair

Figure 366 Group of traveller ladies in a coffee shop at Appleby

Figure 367 A Gypsy family at Appleby

Figure 368 (Left)

Figure 369 (Above)
Travellers at Fell End

Figure 370 (Left)

Figure 371 John and Helen Stephenson. John is the nephew of
Tom Stephenson

The Great Dorset Steam Fair

Figure 372 Dave and Eileen Rawlings with family

Figure 373

Figure 374 Dave Rawlings at Dorset Steam Fair

Figure 375 A group of traveller men at Stow Fair

Figure 376 Stow Fair

Figure 377 Stow Fair

Figure 378 Stow Fair

Figure 379 Stow Fair

Figure 380 Norman Ramshaw and Malcolm Blenkinsop at Appleby

Figure 381 Norman Ramshaw and Malcolm Blenkinsop at Appleby

Figure 382 Arriving at Appleby Fair

Figure 383 Travellers at West Rainton Fair, Co. Durham

Figure 384 Alan Halsall camping at Fell End, Cumbria.
Waiting to pull onto Appleby, 2014

Figure 385 Daren Young near Fell End, Cumbria, 2014

Figure 386 Billy Maguire at Appleby, 2014

Gypsy Convention

Christian Gypsy Convention at Washington, Co. Durham.

Figure 387 Ditty Lee seated with Veronica McKale, young Stephen Lee and two girls, Doll Doll and Scuby Smith

Figure 388 From left to right, Mary Lee, Ditty Lee with baby Stephen Lee, Sandra Coles, Veronica McKale, Christine Douglas and Rose Lee

Chapter 7

Gypsy Living Wagons

There are seven types of Gypsy Wagon and these types varied very little in basic design from the time they were first built. All of these types, with the exception of the Brush Wagon can still be seen at fairs and museums.

The Bow Top Wagon

The Bow Top Wagon has a round canvas top on a bowed frame, the inside of the bow being lined with material. The bow top extends further than the base so that it extends over the wheels, which were large at the back and smaller at the front. The two end walls are made of matchboard with external ribs. This type of wagon was popular with the gypsies because it was light in weight and least likely to turn over because of its low centre of gravity.

However, it was rather dark inside because only one window in the back was possible.

Cheaper versions of this wagon were built where the top was put on an existing trolley or dray, and in these cases the wheels were of more equal size.

Figure 389 The Bow Top Wagon

Square Open Lot

Figure 390 Square Open Lot

This type is similar to the Bow Top, except that the top is square, and therefore windows could be placed in the sides. It was popular amongst New Forest gypsies.

The Reading Wagon

The original design is believed to be by Duntons of Reading, but later it was copied by various builders. It has straight sides which lean out towards the top and is built of matchboarding with external ribs. The wheels at the back are much larger than the front, and run outside the body giving this van a wide wheeltrack of about 7 feet. It has an arched roof and later models had a "lantern" or "mollicroft" introduced into the roof. With the windows in this supplementing the side and rear windows, this type of wagon was very light inside. Nearly all the wagons had some carving on, especially in the form of porch brackets. The amount of carving varied as did the amount of gold leaf applied, the intricacy of the painting and the amount of interior decoration – all according to the purse of the customer. The best of the wagons cost about £800 at the turn of the twentieth century, and when you consider that a house could be built for £300 at that time you begin to realise the amount of work that went into the making of a wagon.

Figure 391 The Reading Wagon   Figure 392 The Ledge Wagon

The Ledge Wagon

Sometimes called the cottage wagon is similar to the Reading, but with a ledge, so that the rear wheels can run underneath the top part of the wagon, thus reducing the wheeltrack of the vehicle.

Spindle cages were built into this space created by the ledge on the outside, to provide more storage space. Like the Reading, later models of this type also had a mollicroft roof. In some of the earlier models this did not run full length.

The Brush Wagon

The Brush was used by brush and basket-makers to sell their wares. Built like the Reading, it was fitted on the outside with glass cases and spindle racks to display their goods. Unlike any other wagon the door was at the back. There is only one or two types of this wagon still in existence in this country.

Figure 393 The Brush Wagon

The Burton Wagon (or Show Man's Wagon)

The Burton was originally built for showmen rather than gypsies, but later became used by them. All four wheels are more or less the same size and are placed under the wagon. This allowed the floor area to be wider, but smaller wheels were not so good on soft ground. It was straight sided with no outward lean like the Reading. There were sub-types of this wagon:

1. Built with matchboarding and ribs, and only one window each side like the Reading.

Figure 394 The Burton Wagon

2. As above but with two windows each side.

3. Of panel construction, very often with ornate carvings on the panels.

All three types had mollicroft roofs.

The Open Lot Wagon

The Open Lot was not actually made until 1930 and is similar in construction to the cheaper Bow Top, in that it was usually built on an existing cart. The main difference is that it is open fronted and has no running board to sit on, as this is not necessary with the open front. It was popular as a summer wagon, and also for use by those gypsies that were house dwellers, but still liked to visit fairs etc, in a wagon.

All these wagons were fitted with a rack called a cratch, for carrying various goods, and underneath at the back is the pan box for all the pots and pans. It is interesting to note that the matchboarding used was either called Penny or Penny Farthing boarding being the width of an old penny and a farthing.

The Wagon Builders

The best known builders in the south were Duntons of Reading, who built fine Reading, Burton and Ledge wagons.

Thomas of Chertsey built mainly for showmen and were noted for their sturdy Burton wagons. Orton and Spooner from Burton on Trent were renowned for their fine carving and built mainly Burtons, but also very good Reading and Ledge wagons.

Figure 395 An open lot wagon at Yarm Fair

Tong of Bolton built the most highly decorated wagons of all, and built all types. In Yorkshire Wright and Hill specialised in Bow Tops, although Wright built Reading and Ledge wagons of high quality as well.

These are perhaps the best known, but there were many other builders too. Some gypsies built their own, which were very often called Peg-Knife wagons, because they claimed to have used no other tool than the knife they used for peg making.

The History of the Living Wagons

The Gypsy Wagon or Vardo as they called it was the gypsies most prized possession, because it was not just a means of transport or holiday home, as the modern caravan is to the house dweller it was their home. It was also the best way that gypsies could show the rest of the world how wealthy they were, much the same way as people today live in the best possible house they can afford.

Until about 1830 gypsies in England roamed the land on foot, carrying their few possessions with them. The better off may have used a pack horse or donkey. They carried with them a piece of canvas which with the aid of poles, was stretched against a bank or hedge and under which they slept. This developed into the bender or bee hive tent because of its shape. Hazel rods were used or ash poles they would be cut on site and bound together to form arches, and canvas or blankets were thrown over them. Many gypsies would sleep in farmer's barns if possible, somewhere that was warm and dry.

About 1830 the roads started to improve, and gypsies began to use pot carts, which were two wheeled to start with, but later became four wheeled. In good weather they would simply sleep under the cart, but some started to use their canvas as a cover for the cart. At first this was erected on simple poles, cut on site as a temporary cover for the period of their stay in one spot, but gradually it became a more permanent feature, and eventually developed into the Bow Top Wagon. The tilt cart would have been used at this time, the shafts would have been pushed through a stout hedge to keep the vehicle level and stable.

It is doubtful if gypsies started using wagons with fitted interiors until about 1870. Even the four wheeled Pot Cart with fitted tilt would have had a stove or furniture fitted inside.

Wagons were built by specialist builders, and gradually took about six months to complete. The better ones could take much longer. The different builders all had their individual style, and an expert can tell even today who built a particular wagon, by such things as the type of porch brackets and crown board, how the axle castings are carved, and how the under works are finished off.

The Interior of the Wagon

The internal layout of the wagon varies very little either between wagons or even different types of wagon. The door is in the front, and of the stable door type. As you go through the door, first there is a tall narrow wardrobe on the left, and the fireplace, which is on this side (the off side) so that the chimney avoids low branches of hedgerow trees. Over the stove is an airing cupboard which the double skinned chimney heats. Beyond the stove is the window with a locker seat underneath. On the right is a china cabinet with a storage cupboard underneath, and then another locker seat and a chest of draws. Across the whole of the back of the wagon is the bed space which can usually be pulled out to form a double bed. Under the bed is another space where children sleep, which if there are no children, used for storage.

The stove was used only for heating, as the cooking was done outside over a wood fire. During the winter and when it was raining the cooking would be done inside. Sometimes a tent was used for cooking this was called a cottage tent or a kitchen tent. Lighting was provided by oil lamps, usually ornate, and the best wagons were fitted with the elaborate Angel Lamps. Gypsies were very fond of ornaments and always had good quality, and the best they could afford – Royal Worcester and Crown Derby China, Cranberry Glass and heavy brass ornaments were among their favourites.

The following are some of the earliest living wagons

Figure 396

Figure 397

Figure 398

Figure 399

Figure 400

Figure 401

Laurel - Originally Built by Orton and Spooner, 1894

This Burton Showman's Wagon was found in the north west of England in a sorry state.

Purchased by the Perks family, it was transported to Shropshire and renovated and completely rebuilt at the wheelwright shop from October 2011-13 by Stewart Whitehead and Richard Connell.

Only a small amount of the original wagon survived. From the under works, the iron work and the lock (turntable) were rescued. The lock needed a lot of carving replacing. To tie the lock and top together, cross beams were added (summers) with carved heads that protrude from the side of the wagon.

The panels from the old wagon were restored and a new panel and ridged top was made. Sash windows replaced the old frames.

The rebuilding of the wagon was done in the same precise way Orton built it in the 1890s. The carvings on the wagon had been cast in resin, they were re-carved in oak by wood carver Alex Finch.

When the wagon came for restoration, oil paintings were found under plywood in the roof, they were badly damaged by water. Photographs were taken of them and Stewart Whitehead repainted new paintings based on the photographs. A few new paintings were added, the basket of fruit in the front of the wagon, four goldfinches and a painting of laurel leaves, with wild flowers in the back bed area.

A new pan box, steps and cratch were also added.

Figure 402

New wooden wheels made from Elm, Oak and Ash were made by Richard Connell at (The Wheelwright Shop). The fireplace surround, drawers and bed came from the original wagon but new boxes and bow fronted cupboard were added to the interior.

This wagon was shown at Malpas Yesteryear Rally in 2013 unpainted.

Over the next year the wagon was painted and lined by Stewart Whitehead. All the carvings, chamfers were gilded in 25.5ct gold leaf by Anthony Perks and Stewart. Finally finished with a few layers of high build varnish. Shutters were made for the bed, from the original.

The shutters were made for the bed from the original scroll designs found on the cupboards and were gilded and painted on the cupboard door and shutters. A new brake system was made by Andrew Smith and a hand rail for the steps.

The restoration of this wagon is all because of a wonderful woman called Laurel Perks who was raised in a wagon herself. Her son Anthony wanted to restore this wagon for her, but sadly she passed away during its restoration.

The carvings on the crown boards bares the name Laurel and is dedicated to her memory.

This old photo found by John Pockett shows the wagon and it could be Orton standing in front of it.

Figure 403 The wagon in its original state

Figure 404

Figure 405 (Left)

Figure 406 (Above)

Figure 407 (Left)

Chris Hughes Bow Top Living Wagon

Three generations of the Hughes family built a gypsy wagon from scratch. Chris and his family have a great love for the Gypsy way of life. The photographs are of the horse drawn wagon that they spent a lot of time producing. Well done!

Figure 408

Figure 409 Three generations of skilled men

Figure 410
The Bow Top wagon that Chris, his father and grandfather built

Figure 411

Chapter 8

Not A Big Fat Gypsy Wedding

The Wedding of Nina Lee and Zacc Burton at Hardwick Hall, County Durham, 2014

Figure 412 Zacc and Nina Burton on their wedding day

Figure 413

Figure 414

Figure 415 Group of men when signing the register

Figure 416 Group of people when signing the register

Figure 417 Bride and Bridesmaids

Figure 418 Yoke of horse and dray

Figure 419 (Above)

Figure 420 (Below)
Zacc and the Best Man

Figure 421 (Above)
Mum and Dad Lee with Nina

Figure 422 (Left)
Mum and Dad Burton with Zacc

Figure 423 Mr and Mrs Burton

Chapter 9

Gypsy Artists

Diana Rosemary Lodge : Artist of Rural and Gypsy Life

Diana is a native of Upper Wharfedale and has been painting from a very early age. After receiving her education at Burnsall Primary and Skipton Girls High School she graduated to Harrogate Art College.

Living in the heart of the Yorkshire Dales has provided her with unlimited opportunities for colourful landscape painting, but with a passionate love of horses it was almost inevitable that they should constitute important subjects for her work. Whilst still young she acquired her own Gypsy Wagon – a typical Open Lot – and with a life-long interest in Gypsies and their way of life, pictures of Romany scenes have become her speciality and for which she is well known. Rosemary's work is in private collections, mainly in England and also in Canada, Australia, New Zealand and on the continent.

Diana can be contacted on 01756 720668 or 07751 075307 if you are interested in purchasing any of her artwork.

Figure 424 Diana Rosemary Lodge at Appleby Fair

Figure 425 (Above)
Rosemary Lodge with one of her daughters Kizzy, in a wagon built by Joe Thompson (Barras), Thinford, Co. Durham. This photograph was taken at Hubberholme. Kizzy is now 29 and is a Doctor working in Aberdeen, Scotland.

Figure 426 (Right)
Rosemary and her living wagon

Figure 427 (Left)
Rosemary painting at Appletreewick
(Upper Wharfedale), Yorkshire

Figure 428 (Below)
Rosemary and her two horses, Paddy
and Danny

Figure 429 Rosemary's Mother
'This is a picture of my Mum when she was 19. She had just had to have her hair cut short after she had diphtheria. Her hair was so long she could sit on it.' Rosemary said her Mum was a real Romany lady

Figure 430 (Left)

Figure 431 (Below)

Figure 432 (Above)
Harry Monroe with Winston
and Ted

Figure 433 (Right)
'Fireside chat' with Frank Williams
and Paddy the horse

Figure 434 (Above)

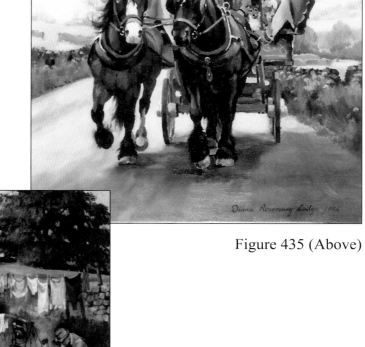

Figure 435 (Above)

Figure 436 (Above)

Figure 437 (Right)

Paintings by Sir Alfred Munnings

Figure 438 Painting of Epsom Downs

Figure 439 Painting of Epsom Downs

Figure 440 Gypsy Horse Fair

Figure 441 Epsom Downs

Paintings by Dame Laura Knight (1877 - 1970)

Laura Knight was one of the leading women artists of the twentieth century, she was a household name during her lifetime and the first woman artist to be made Dame of the British Empire. Her work is remarkable both for its variety and for its quality.

She is perhaps most famous for her captivating portrayals of the London theatre and ballet, also the circus. Laura also had a great love for the gypsies and many of her paintings were done in gypsy camps or at the races such as Ascot and the Derby.

Some of her paintings of gypsy life are portrayed on the next few pages.

Figure 442 The Hop Picker (Granny Knowles)
See Figure 1 at the front of the book, Granny Smith titled 'Gypsy Splendour'

At Epsom, Laura became friendly with an elderly gypsy woman known as 'Granny Smith', who invited her to visit their camp. Laura visited the gypsy camp regularly every weekday. The gypsies were happy to pose for Laura and she was able to produce a number of extremely sensitive portraits as a result.

This is perhaps one of the most outstanding gypsy paintings of the old gypsy granny wearing all her best clothes, entitled gypsy splendour. Her vigorous but sensitive handling of paint has lent itself particularly well to portraying this wrinkled old lady. One feels that whatever life has dealt her, including her broken nose (as she told Laura: 'It was me 'usband, twice!'), nothing disturbed her dignified calm.

Figure 443 (Left)

Figure 444 (Below)

Figure 445 (Above)

Figure 446 (Right)

Figure 447 (Above)

Figure 448 (Right)

Figure 449